INSIDE THE
NFL

DETROIT
LIONS

BY WILLIAM MEIER

SportsZone

An Imprint of Abdo Publishing
abdobooks.com

abdobooks.com

Published by Abdo Publishing, a division of ABDO, PO Box 398166, Minneapolis, Minnesota 55439. Copyright © 2020 by Abdo Consulting Group, Inc. International copyrights reserved in all countries. No part of this book may be reproduced in any form without written permission from the publisher. SportsZone™ is a trademark and logo of Abdo Publishing.

Printed in the United States of America, North Mankato, Minnesota
022019
092019

THIS BOOK CONTAINS
RECYCLED MATERIALS

Cover Photo: Kevin Terrell/AP Images
Interior Photos: Marvin E. Newmann/Sports Illustrated/Getty Images, 5, 7, 9, 43; NFL Photos/AP Images, 11, 22, 29; AP Images, 13, 33; George Gelatly/Getty Images Sport/ Getty Images, 15, 16; Walter Stein/AP Images, 19; PS/AP Images, 21; Peter Read Miller/ AP Images, 24; Focus on Sport/Getty Images Sport/Getty Images, 27; Tom Pidgeon/AP Images, 31; Morry Gash/AP Images, 35; Paul Sancya/AP Images, 37, 38; Duane Burleson/ AP Images, 40

Editor: Patrick Donnelly
Series Designer: Craig Hinton

Library of Congress Control Number: 2018965347

Publisher's Cataloging-in-Publication Data

Names: Meier, William, author.
Title: Detroit Lions / by William Meier
Description: Minneapolis, Minnesota: Abdo Publishing, 2020 | Series: Inside the NFL | Includes online resources and index.
Identifiers: ISBN 9781532118463 (lib. bdg.) | ISBN 9781532172649 (ebook)
Subjects: LCSH: Detroit Lions (Football team)--Juvenile literature. | National Football League--Juvenile literature. | Football teams--Juvenile literature. | American football—Juvenile literature.
Classification: DDC 796.33264--dc23

TABLE OF
CONTENTS

CHAPTER 1
THEY ONCE WERE CHAMPIONS... 4

CHAPTER 2
THE EARLY YEARS.................. 10

CHAPTER 3
LION KINGS NO LONGER.......... 20

CHAPTER 4
BARRY'S BUNCH.................. 26

CHAPTER 5
ROCK BOTTOM AND REBOUND .. 34

TIMELINE   42
QUICK STATS   44
QUOTES AND ANECDOTES   45
GLOSSARY   46
MORE INFORMATION   47
ONLINE RESOURCES   47
INDEX   48
ABOUT THE AUTHOR   48

THEY ONCE WERE CHAMPIONS

The 1957 season started with a shock for the Detroit Lions. But they finished the season with a mighty roar. On December 29 of that year, they crushed the Cleveland Browns 59–14 to win the National Football League (NFL) Championship Game.

Lions quarterback Tobin Rote threw four touchdown passes and ran for another score that day. He completed 12 of 19 passes for 280 yards. Detroit held Cleveland's star running back Jim Brown to 69 rushing yards on 20 carries. The 55,263 fans in attendance at Briggs Stadium in Detroit were proud of their Lions.

It was an amazing ending that few fans could have imagined just a few months earlier. Buddy Parker had

Lions star Yale Lary punts the ball against the Cleveland Browns during the 1957 NFL Championship Game.

coached the Lions to NFL titles in 1952 and 1953. But during training camp in August 1957, he sent shockwaves throughout the league by announcing that he was quitting.

The Lions named assistant coach George Wilson the new head coach. Most people, including Detroit's players, liked Wilson. But few people had confidence in him as a head coach in the NFL.

Rote was also new to the team in 1957. The Lions had acquired the longtime Green Bay Packers quarterback in a trade before the season. That gave them a strong second option in case Bobby Layne, Detroit's starter at the position since 1950, got hurt or struggled.

Layne was popular in Detroit. However, the Lions had failed to win the conference title in 1956, in large part because Layne had gotten hurt in the season finale against the Chicago Bears.

BUDDY PARKER

Lions coach Buddy Parker came up with many innovations. He was the first coach to have his players stay together in a hotel the night before home games. This was done to help them focus on the coming game without any distractions. He shortened practices, loosened rules for players, and was credited with starting the "two-minute offense." In the two-minute offense, the team lines up without huddling and the quarterback calls the play at the line of scrimmage. This allows the offense to run more plays when time is running out.

✕ The Lions didn't give Jim Brown much room to run during the 1957 NFL Championship Game.

That led to Detroit's decision to acquire Rote. Layne was not happy to have new competition for the position.

Detroit won six of its first 10 games in 1957. The Lions were in the race for the conference title with two games left. The next game was against Cleveland at Briggs Stadium. In the second quarter, Layne dropped back to pass. But the Browns' Don Colo and Paul Wiggin smashed into Layne, breaking

TOBIN ROTE

Quarterback Tobin Rote was selected seventeenth overall by the Green Bay Packers in the 1950 NFL Draft. During his seven years in Green Bay, he ranked third in the NFL in passing touchdowns and first in rushing yards by a quarterback. In 1956 the Packers went 4–8. But Rote led the league in passing yards (2,203) and touchdown passes (18). He also rushed for 11 touchdowns. After the 1956 season, Green Bay traded Rote to Detroit, where he led the Lions to the 1957 title. He held the starting job through the 1959 season, then finished his career with stints in Canada and in the rival American Football League (AFL). He retired after playing for the AFL's Denver Broncos in 1966.

several bones in his ankle and lower leg. This was devastating for Layne, but the exact situation the Lions had planned for. Rote took over at quarterback and led Detroit to a 20–7 win at Cleveland.

The Lions then went on to beat the Chicago Bears 21–13 in the regular-season finale. That put Detroit in a tie with the San Francisco 49ers for the NFL Western Conference title. The teams met in a one-game playoff to decide who would advance to the NFL Championship Game. The visiting Lions trailed 27–7 in the third quarter, but they rallied with 24 unanswered points to beat the 49ers 31–27.

Detroit followed that victory with the big title-game win over Cleveland. It was a joyous time in Michigan. Unfortunately, Lions

Quarterback Tobin Rote (18) throws a pass against the Browns in the 1957 NFL Championship Game.

fans are still waiting for their team to match that level of success. Through 2018 the Lions had yet to win another NFL championship, which has been called the Super Bowl since the 1966 season. In fact, Detroit had won only one playoff game since 1957.

There was a time when the Lions were one of the most feared teams in the league. But with just a single postseason victory in more than 60 seasons, they have endured one of the most frustrating and least successful stretches of play for a team in NFL history. That was not what radio executive George A. Richards had in mind when he purchased the Portsmouth (Ohio) Spartans in 1933 for $8,000–an astounding price tag at the time–and moved the team to Detroit.

CHAPTER 2

THE EARLY YEARS

Before becoming the Detroit Lions, the team began in 1929 as the Spartans, based in Portsmouth, Ohio. They gained membership in the young NFL for the 1930 season and became a title contender immediately.

The Spartans and the Chicago Bears ended the 1932 season with six wins and one loss each. The NFL championship had previously been awarded to the team with the best record in the league. But since the Spartans and the Bears were tied, they played each other in the first NFL title game.

Although the Spartans lost 9–0, the game was so successful that the NFL decided to repeat it. The next year, the league realigned into two divisions. The Eastern Division

Future Pro Football Hall of Famer Earl "Dutch" Clark played for the Lions from 1934 to 1938.

IRON MAN GAME

Portsmouth played an "iron man" game against Green Bay in 1932. Spartans coach Potsy Clark refused to make a single substitution. Portsmouth won 19–0 while using only 11 players.

winner would meet the Western Division winner in the annual NFL Championship Game.

After the 1933 season, Detroit radio executive George A. Richards bought the Spartans and moved the team to Detroit. He renamed the team after the "king of the jungle" because he wanted them to be the kings of the NFL.

The Lions won their first NFL title in 1935. They beat the New York Giants 26–7 in the championship game. Quarterback Earl "Dutch" Clark led the way for Detroit. He ran for a 40-yard touchdown. Clark was considered a triple threat on offense— he was an effective passer, runner, and drop kicker.

The Lions enjoyed some early success during their first several seasons in Detroit. The 1940s were more challenging. They won only 35 of 110 games that decade. In 1942 Detroit went 0–11. The team had only five touchdowns all season and did not score more than seven points in any game. In 1943 the host Lions played the Giants in a game that ended in a 0–0 tie.

Doak Walker joined the Lions in 1950. Today, the Doak Walker Award honors the nation's top college running back each year.

The Lions managed winning seasons in 1944 and 1945. But from 1946 to 1949, the Lions won just a total of 10 games. The team's fans were looking forward to a new decade. The 1950s would turn out to be much more successful.

In 1950 the Lions drafted running back Doak Walker. They also picked up quarterback Bobby Layne in a trade with the New York Bulldogs. After Detroit finished 6–6, head coach

Alvin "Bo" McMillin resigned. Assistant Buddy Parker was promoted to head coach in 1951. He had played for the Lions as a fullback. He even helped them win the 1935 NFL title. Detroit's greatest era had begun.

The Lions got close in Parker's first season as head coach. They went 7–4–1 to finish just a half game behind the Los Angeles Rams in the National Conference. Los Angeles went on to win the NFL title.

Detroit would get revenge on the Rams in 1952. After a shaky 1–2 start that season, the Lions won nine of their final 10 games in the regular season. The Rams and Lions each finished with 9–3 records.

Behind two rushing touchdowns from fullback Pat Harder, the Lions beat the visiting Rams 31–21 in a playoff game

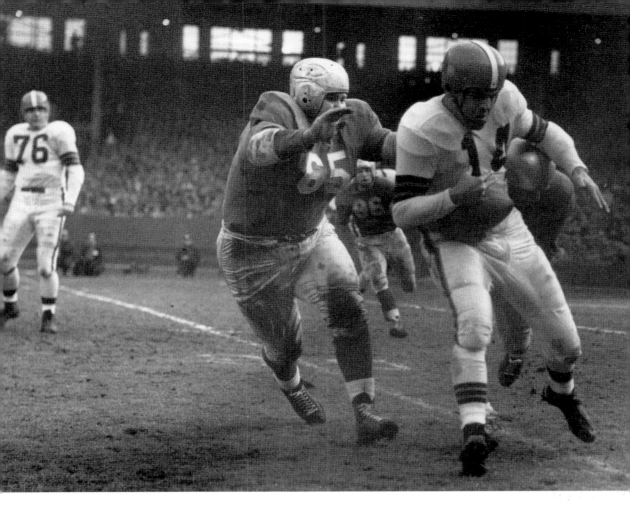

Two Lions bring down Cleveland Browns quarterback Otto Graham during the 1952 NFL Championship Game.

to determine the National Conference champion. Then they played the American Conference champion Cleveland Browns in the NFL Championship Game on December 28. In subfreezing temperatures, the visiting Lions faced the Browns and their star quarterback, Otto Graham. Early in the second quarter, Layne scored on a 2-yard run. Then, in the third

Linebacker Joe Schmidt, *left*, and tackle Lou Creekmur carry coach Buddy Parker off the field after the 1953 NFL Championship Game.

quarter, Walker rumbled 67 yards for a touchdown. That gave Detroit a 14–0 lead.

Cleveland's Chick Jagade found the end zone on a 7-yard run in the third quarter. That brought the Browns within seven points. But Harder added a 36-yard field goal in the fourth quarter to put Detroit ahead 17–7. The Lions held on to win by that score, giving them their second NFL title.

The Lions did not slow down after that. They won their final six games of the 1953 season to finish with a 10–2 record and win the Western Conference title. Detroit again faced Cleveland in the NFL Championship Game, this time at Detroit's Briggs Stadium.

It turned out to be a game for the ages. The score was tied 10–10 after three quarters. The Browns kicked two field goals to take a 16–10 lead. With 4:10 left, the Lions took over at their own 20-yard line. Layne quickly moved the ball into Cleveland territory. Layne then found Jim Doran for a perfectly thrown 33-yard touchdown pass with 2:08 remaining. Walker kicked the extra point to give Detroit a 17–16 lead, and the Lions held on to win their second straight NFL title.

The next season, the Lions finished 9–2–1 and again won the Western Conference crown. And once again, they met Cleveland in the NFL title game. This time, though, the host Browns dominated the favored Lions 56–10.

The hangover from that drubbing lasted into the next year. Layne hurt his right shoulder before the 1955 season and had trouble throwing. The team finished with an NFL-worst 3–9 record. Several Lions retired, including Walker, their star running back and place kicker.

But Layne and the Lions were back on track in 1956. They opened the season with a six-game winning streak. They closed it by visiting the Chicago Bears in the final week with the Western Conference title on the line. Chicago won 38–21 and earned the championship.

In the Bears game, Layne had been knocked out by a hit from behind. Layne's injury led Detroit to trade for quarterback Tobin Rote before the 1957 season. Parker quit as coach before that season and was replaced by George Wilson. The Lions went on to win their third NFL championship of the decade.

Layne was determined to play in 1958. In the second game of the season, Detroit and Green Bay tied 13–13. Layne—who also kicked extra points—missed one that would have given the Lions the win. The next day, Layne received a call from Wilson. He had been traded to Pittsburgh, where he would be coached by a familiar face, Buddy Parker. Layne boarded

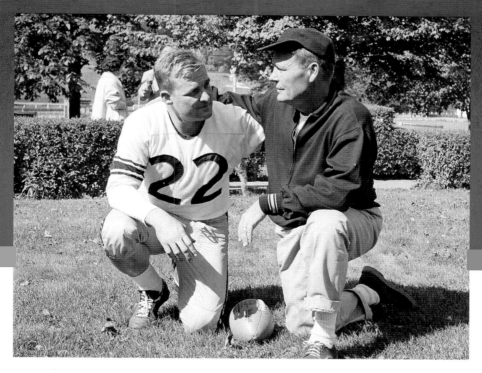

Bobby Layne, *left*, and Parker huddle at practice in Pittsburgh the day after Parker acquired Layne from the Lions.

a plane that night and joined Parker at Steelers practice the next day.

On his way out of Detroit, Layne reportedly said the Lions would "not win for 50 years." This prediction proved to be true, as far as NFL titles go. It's often referred to as "the Curse of Bobby Layne." Detroit finished 4–7–1 in 1958 and dropped to 3–8–1 the next year. This closed the book on a wildly successful decade and set the stage for a long run of disappointment in Detroit.

CHAPTER 3

LION KINGS
NO LONGER

The Lions experienced some big roster changes in the late 1950s. But that did not stop the team from winning. The Lions finished second in the Western Conference in 1960, 1961, and 1962. During those years, defense was Detroit's strength.

Linebacker Joe Schmidt excelled at rushing the quarterback. Safety Yale Lary made 50 interceptions during his career with the Lions. Cornerback Dick "Night Train" Lane was known for hitting the opposition ball carriers high and hard. But perhaps the most frightening Lion was 250-pound defensive tackle Alex Karras. He was strong, relentless, and very fast. Offensive linemen feared him. Sometimes even running backs could not match his speed.

Dick "Night Train" Lane leaps to break up a pass intended for Baltimore Colts receiver Jimmy Orr during a 1962 win.

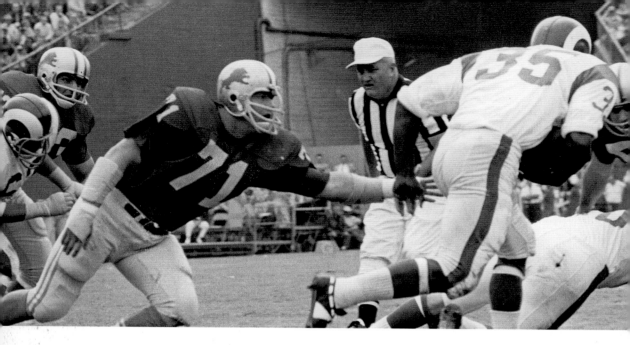

Lions defensive tackle Alex Karras reaches out to tackle a Los Angeles Rams player in 1968.

The Lions drafted Karras out of the University of Iowa in 1958. Just before he had signed a professional wrestling contract that earned him $25,000 during the six-month offseason.

Karras's wrestling background served him well in 1963. That January, the NFL questioned his ownership in the Lindell AC Bar in Detroit. There had been reports that the bar was home to gambling and the presence of organized crime. Karras was urged to sell his share of the business. He first threatened to retire from football. He then admitted to placing bets on NFL games. The league suspended him for one season. Karras returned to pro wrestling for the year.

NFL commissioner Pete Rozelle reinstated Karras for the 1964 season. During that season, an official asked Karras to call the pregame coin toss for his team. "I'm sorry, sir," Karras replied. "I'm not permitted to gamble."

Karras verbally sparred with the Lions' coaches. He asked to be traded in 1964. He threatened to sign with the expansion Miami Dolphins of the AFL in 1966. He then hinted that he might retire early. But through it all, he remained with Detroit. He retired in 1970 at age 35 and began a long and successful career as an actor.

PAPER LION

In 1963 sportswriter George Plimpton joined the Lions for their training camp at a private school near Bloomfield Hills, Michigan. The result of his experiences is chronicled in the book *Paper Lion: Confessions of a Last-String Quarterback*. Plimpton wore No. 0 and participated in a Lions scrimmage at Wisner Stadium in Pontiac, Michigan. He netted minus-29 yards in his five plays as quarterback. Plimpton, then 36 years old, wanted to show how difficult it would be for an average person to succeed in the NFL. The book is considered a sports literature classic.

The Lions of the 1960s had several other talented players besides Karras, even if they did not make as many newspaper headlines. Dick LeBeau and Lem Barney were standout defensive backs. Both would be enshrined in the Pro Football Hall of Fame. So would tight end Charlie Sanders. The team had drafted him in 1968. Linebacker Wayne Walker and center

Lions running back Billy Sims rushed for 153 yards and three touchdowns against the Rams in his first pro game in 1980.

Ed Flanagan were other players who received frequent Pro Bowl selections.

Detroit had several losing seasons in the 1960s, however. The Lions did not reach the playoffs at all that decade. The 1970s would not be much different.

The Lions only made the playoffs once in the 1970s, and that was in 1970. Detroit lost 5–0 to the Dallas Cowboys in the first round. That was the lowest-scoring playoff game in NFL history. From 1970 to 1978, the Lions placed either second or third every year in their division.

Detroit bottomed out in 1979, finishing with the worst record in the league at 2–14. That gave the team the first pick in the 1980 NFL Draft. The Lions used the pick to select Heisman Trophy-winning running back Billy Sims from the University of Oklahoma. Sims was an immediate hit. He rushed for a team-record 1,303 yards and scored 16 touchdowns total en route to winning the NFL Rookie of the Year Award in 1980.

With Sims leading the way, the Lions made the playoffs in 1982. The next year they won their first division title since 1957. However, Detroit lost in the first round of the postseason both times. Washington, the eventual Super Bowl champion, beat Detroit 31–7 in 1982. The host San Francisco 49ers and quarterback Joe Montana edged the Lions 24–23 in the divisional round in 1983. Detroit's Eddie Murray missed a 43-yard field-goal try with five seconds left.

Then disaster struck. Sims was well on his way to another dominating year when he suffered a serious knee injury midway through the 1984 season. This ended his career just as it was taking off. It also hurt Detroit's prospects of success. The Lions would not manage a record over .500 for the rest of the decade. Thankfully for Lions fans, a new star running back was on the way soon.

CHAPTER 4

BARRY'S BUNCH

In the 1989 NFL Draft, the Lions selected running back Barry Sanders with the third overall pick. He helped make the 1990s one of the most interesting and successful eras in team history. Detroit reached the playoffs six times during the decade. With his breakaway speed and amazing ability to elude defenders, Sanders became known as one of the best running backs in NFL history.

Sanders won the Heisman Trophy for his 1988 season at Oklahoma State University. He rushed for a college-record 2,628 yards and scored 39 touchdowns that year. Sanders was only 5 feet 8 inches tall. But he had a combination of great balance, vision, and strength. His ability to spin, juke, and cut was unmatched in the game.

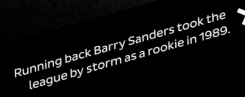

Running back Barry Sanders took the league by storm as a rookie in 1989.

HUMBLE HERO

Lions running back Barry Sanders decided to wear No. 20 as a rookie. Former star running back Billy Sims had worn that same number with Detroit. Sanders rushed for 1,470 yards in 1989, 10 yards short of the NFL rushing title. Sanders could have passed Kansas City's Christian Okoye in the final game of the season. But he chose not to go back into a game that the Lions had control of in the fourth quarter. "Coach, let's just win it and go home," he reportedly said. Despite being one of the NFL's top players, Sanders did not have a big ego. He was known for politely handing the ball to a referee after he scored touchdowns instead of calling attention to himself with a celebratory dance.

Sanders finished with 1,470 rushing yards in 1989. He was named the NFL Offensive Rookie of the Year. Sanders also broke Billy Sims's Lions rookie rushing record. He went on to rush for a combined 8,672 yards in his first six years in the NFL. He was selected to the Pro Bowl in each of those seasons. Fans loved to watch him make defenders look foolish with his elusive running style.

Detroit strengthened the rest of the team around Sanders. The defense included talented linebackers Chris Spielman and Tracy Scroggins. Bennie Blades was a hard-hitting safety. Sanders had a seven-time Pro Bowl player, Lomas Brown, at offensive tackle to open holes for him. At wide receiver, Brett Perriman combined speed with precise route running. And Herman Moore had been an outstanding high jumper on the track-and-field team at the

✗ Wide receiver Willie Green caught eight passes for 115 yards and two touchdowns as the Lions defeated the Cowboys in a January 1992 playoff game.

University of Virginia. At 6-foot-4, the wide receiver was able to outleap defenders for high passes.

With a retooled roster, the Lions finally ended a long period of mediocrity. The 1991 team went 12–4 and won the NFC Central Division. Then they picked up the franchise's first playoff victory since 1957. Detroit defeated visiting Dallas 38–6 in a divisional-round game on January 5, 1992. But for the second time in 10 years, the Lions were knocked out of the playoffs by Washington, who went on to win the Super Bowl.

The 1993 Lions lost 28–24 to the visiting Green Bay Packers in a wild-card playoff game. Sanders rushed for 169 yards, but

A BIG THUMBS UP

On November 17, 1991, Lions guard Mike Utley suffered a career-ending spinal injury in a game against the Los Angeles Rams. As Utley was carted off the field, he flashed a thumbs-up sign to his teammates and the crowd at the Silverdome. This became a rallying symbol for the remainder of the season.

the Packers won on a 40-yard fourth-quarter touchdown pass from Brett Favre to Sterling Sharpe.

While the Lions offense had relied heavily on Sanders, they'd been making do with a series of journeymen quarterbacks. Before the 1994 season, the Lions tried to address their quarterback issues once and for all. Scott Mitchell had spent three seasons in Miami backing up Dan Marino and had put up some big numbers in 1993 filling in for the injured Hall of Famer. The Lions signed Mitchell to a huge free-agent contract and installed him as their starter.

Mitchell had a rocky start in Detroit. The Lions were 4–5 in early November, and Mitchell had completed just 48 percent of his passes. Veteran Dave Krieg stepped in, and Detroit rallied to finish the season 9–7 and make the playoffs. But the Lions lost in the wild-card round to the Packers again. This time it was 16–12 in Green Bay. Sanders was held to minus-1 yard on 13 carries.

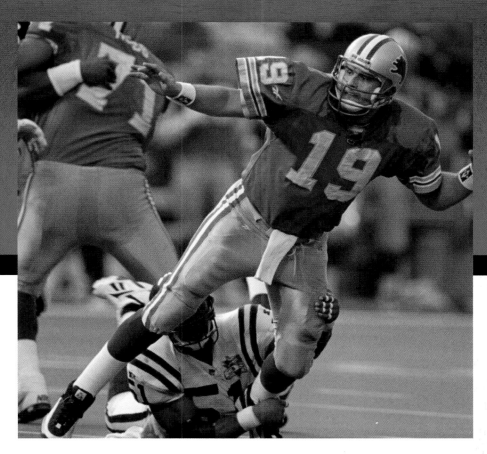

Quarterback Scott Mitchell gets rid of the ball before a Minnesota Vikings defender tackles him during a 1995 game.

In 1995 the Lions lost six of their first nine games. Team owner William Clay Ford Sr. issued an ultimatum: make the playoffs, or there would be big changes, starting with head coach Wayne Fontes.

The Lions responded well. Mitchell passed for 410 yards and four touchdowns to lead Detroit to a 44–38 win over the

Minnesota Vikings on Thanksgiving Day. Mitchell broke Bobby Layne's 45-year-old team record of 374 passing yards in a game.

The Lions won their final seven regular-season games in 1995 to finish 10–6. That also earned them a wild-card spot in the playoffs. Dreams of the Super Bowl did not materialize, though. The visiting Lions lost 58–37 to the Philadelphia Eagles. It was the highest-scoring playoff game in NFL history at the time.

Fontes was given one more year to see if he could take the Lions to the next level. Instead, they went 5–11 and he was fired. Bobby Ross replaced Fontes as the Lions' head coach in 1997. Ross had just spent five years in San Diego, where his Chargers teams never had a losing season and reached the Super Bowl after the 1994 season.

In Ross's first year, Sanders was at his best. He racked up 2,053 rushing yards to become the third player in NFL history to rush for 2,000 yards in a season. The Lions finished the season 9–7. However, they lost 20–10 to the host Tampa Bay Buccaneers in a wild-card playoff game. The Bucs held Sanders to 65 yards on 18 carries.

After another 5–11 season in 1998, Sanders shocked the football world by retiring the next summer. He was only

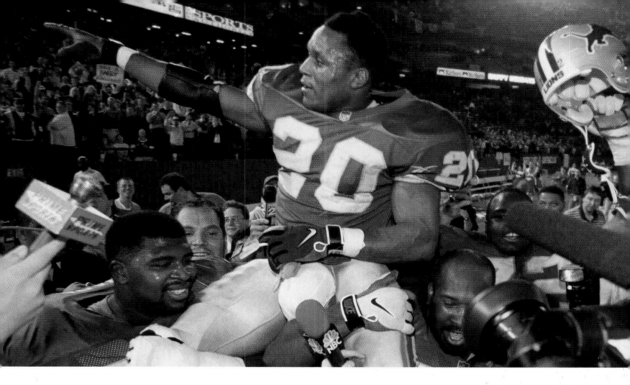

Lions players carry Sanders off the field after he rushed for 184 yards and the game-winning touchdown against the New York Jets in 1997.

31 years old and needed just 1,457 yards to pass former Chicago Bears star Walter Payton as the NFL's all-time leading rusher. He later said he was exhausted by all the losing and frustrated that Lions management didn't do more to build a winning team.

The 1999 Lions finished 8–8 but still reached the postseason. This gave Detroit six playoff teams in the 1990s. That set a team record for the most playoff appearances in a 10-year span. Detroit lost again, though, falling 27–13 at Washington in the wild-card round. That would be a bad omen for the decade to come.

ROCK BOTTOM AND REBOUND

The 2000 Lions finished the season 9–7. They lost their final game 23–20 to the visiting Chicago Bears on a late field goal. As a result, Detroit did not make the playoffs. Unfortunately for the Lions, it would be their best season of the decade.

Detroit vice chairman William Clay Ford Jr. hired former Pro Bowl linebacker Matt Millen as the team's president and CEO in January 2001. Millen would be responsible for building the team into a winner by deciding which players were on the roster. Millen had won four Super Bowls as a player. But he had no front-office experience.

Hiring Millen proved to be a disaster. During his seven seasons in control, the Lions went 31–81 and had the NFL's worst winning percentage at .277. They did not have

Quarterback Dan Orlovsky walks off the field after Detroit became the first team to go winless in a 16-game season.

a winning season. They never finished higher than third place in their division.

One of the main reasons Lions fans were angry at Millen was the team's lack of drafting success. In 2002 the team selected former University of Oregon quarterback Joey Harrington with the third overall pick. Harrington became Detroit's starter almost immediately. But his time with the Lions, from 2002 to 2005, was unsuccessful. Millen also made the unusual choice to select wide receivers in the first round three straight years—Charles Rogers (2003), Roy Williams (2004), and Mike Williams (2005). Roy Williams had some decent moments. But Mike Williams and Rogers were busts.

Partly because of these poor draft decisions, Detroit had a hard time improving on the field. If Bobby Layne did put a 50-year curse on the Lions, it expired with the 2008 season. But instead of winning a championship, the Lions hit rock bottom. Millen was fired after the team lost its first three games.

✕ *From left to right:* wide receivers Roy Williams, Mike Williams, and Charles Rogers never lived up to expectations in Detroit.

Millen's firing, however, did not improve the results on the field. In fact, Detroit lost all 16 of its games in 2008. It was the first time an NFL team finished 0–16. Tampa Bay had gone 0–14 in 1976. The league went to a 16-game schedule in 1978.

Rod Marinelli was fired as coach the day after the season ended. During his three seasons in charge, the Lions went

✕ Lions receiver Calvin Johnson was an explosive threat for the Lions.

10–38. The Lions hired Jim Schwartz as his replacement. Schwartz had been the Tennessee Titans' defensive coordinator. He had helped the Titans go 13–3 in 2008.

The rebuilding process continued with the 2009 NFL Draft. The Lions selected quarterback Matthew Stafford with the number one overall pick. The Lions broke a 19-game losing streak on September 27, 2009. They beat Washington 19–14 at Ford Field. The Lions won only one other game in 2009.

Still, there were some positive signs for the Lions as the 2009 season came to an end. Stafford and star wide receiver

Calvin Johnson seemed to be forming a solid combination. The Lions had drafted Johnson second overall in 2007. He was one bright spot in the 2008 winless season, catching a league-leading 12 touchdown passes and racking up 1,331 yards. Nicknamed "Megatron," Johnson became an elite NFL receiver. With him and Stafford, the Lions developed one of the best offenses in the NFL. After a 6–10 season in 2010, the Lions broke through to the playoffs with a 10–6 record in 2011. They also set a team record with 474 points scored that season.

MEGATRON

Calvin Johnson retired in 2015 as by far the best receiver in Lions history. He is the team's all-time leader in catches, receiving yards, and receiving touchdowns. Johnson is the only Lion to top 10,000 career receiving yards.

The Lions lost at New Orleans in the first round of the playoffs, but they finally looked like they had the makings of a contender. Instead, they took another step back. Their scoring output dropped by more than 100 points in 2012. After starting 4–4, they lost their last eight in a row and finished 4–12. After another losing season in 2013, Schwartz was fired.

In came former Indianapolis Colts head coach Jim Caldwell. The Lions bounced back right away under Caldwell and finished 11–5, their best record since 1991. Thanks in part to the dominance of defensive lineman Ndamukong Suh, the

✖ Quarterback Matthew Stafford tries to shake off a Bears tackler in 2018.

Lions surrendered the second-fewest yards in the NFL. But again, they lost in the first round of the playoffs with a 24–20 heartbreaker at Dallas.

After a 7–9 season in 2015, the Lions suffered a shocking loss. Johnson suddenly announced his retirement at age 30. Much like Sanders, he retired at the top of his game.

Still, having Stafford meant the Lions remained competitive. They made another playoff appearance after a 9–7 season in 2016 but were drubbed by Seattle in the wild-card round. Stafford couldn't do it alone. The Lions were caught in a cycle of mediocrity.

To change that, they parted ways with Caldwell after the 2017 season. They hired Matt Patricia, the defensive coordinator for the New England Patriots. Patricia had won three Super Bowls while on the New England staff. Lions fans hoped that he could work similar magic in Detroit. However, a 6–10 season in 2018 showed the team still had a ways to go to catch up to the rest of the league and remind their fans of their championship pedigree.

QB CONNECTION

In early 2009, Matthew Stafford received a phone call from his mother asking, "Have you heard the story about Bobby Layne?" Though Stafford knew nothing about the "curse," he knew plenty about Layne. That is because Stafford had walked past two plaques at the entrance to Highland Park High School Stadium before each game for four years. Stafford played for the same high school in Dallas, Texas, as former Lions greats Layne and Doak Walker had in the 1940s. In 2005 Stafford led Highland Park to its first state championship in nearly 50 years.

TIMELINE

The Portsmouth Spartans, based in Portsmouth, Ohio, begin play as an independent professional team. They join the NFL one year later.

1929

The Spartans, having been purchased by George A. Richards, are moved to Detroit and renamed the Lions.

1934

Quarterback Dutch Clark leads the Lions to a 26–7 win over the New York Giants in the NFL Championship Game.

1935

Behind quarterback Bobby Layne, the Lions win their second NFL championship, 17–7 over the Cleveland Browns.

1952

The Lions finish 10–2 and earn another spot in the NFL Championship Game. They again defeat the Browns—this time 17–16 in Detroit.

1953

Detroit makes another trip to the NFL Championship Game against Cleveland. But the host Browns roll to a 56–10 win.

1954

The Lions advance to yet another NFL title game against the Browns. Detroit crushes Cleveland 59–14 in front of 55,263 fans at Briggs Stadium.

1957

Bobby Layne is traded to the Pittsburgh Steelers. On his way out of Detroit, Layne reportedly said the Lions would "not win for 50 years."

1958

The Lions qualify for the playoffs as the NFC's wild card, the team's first postseason berth since 1957. Detroit loses 5–0 to the Dallas Cowboys.

1970

The Lions begin a new era by playing their home games in the Silverdome in the Detroit suburb of Pontiac, Michigan.

1975

The Lions capture their first division championship since 1957. The host San Francisco 49ers beat the Lions 24–23 in the first round of the playoffs.

✕

1983

Star running back Billy Sims suffers a devastating knee injury and is forced to retire at age 29.

✕

1984

The Lions defeat the visiting Dallas Cowboys in the divisional round of the playoffs on January 5.

✕

1992

Barry Sanders runs for 2,053 yards, becoming only the third player in NFL history to reach 2,000 rushing yards in a season.

✕

1997

Sanders retires before training camp. He is 31 years old and still in the prime of his career.

✕

1999

The Lions move into a new stadium, Ford Field, in downtown Detroit.

✕

2002

The Lions finish the season 0–16, becoming the first team to go winless since the NFL went to a 16-game schedule in 1978.

✕

2008

Detroit finishes with a record of 11–5, its best record in 23 years.

✕

2014

Calvin Johnson retires as the Lions' all-time leader in catches, receiving yards, and receiving touchdowns.

✕

2015

The Lions cap a 6–10 year under rookie head coach Matt Patricia with a 31–0 win at Green Bay on December 30.

✕

2018

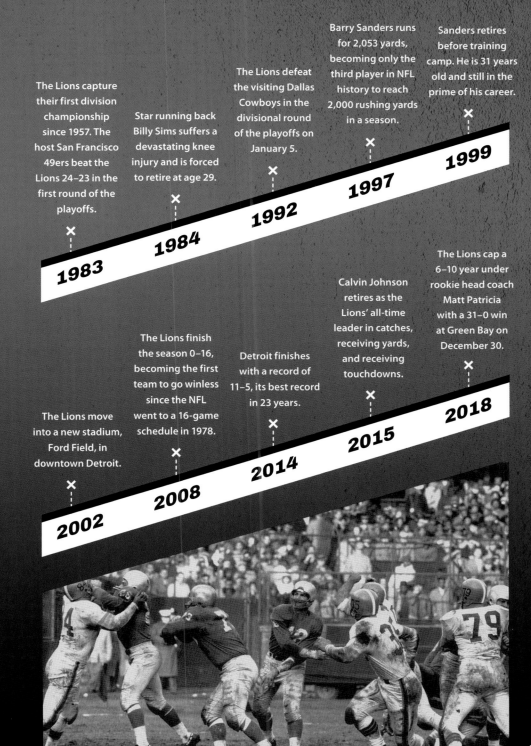

QUICK STATS

FRANCHISE HISTORY

Portsmouth Spartans (1930–33)
Detroit Lions (1934–)

SUPER BOWLS

None

NFL CHAMPIONSHIP GAMES *(1933–69, wins in bold)*

1935, **1952**, **1953**, 1954, **1957**

NFC CHAMPIONSHIP GAMES (SINCE 1970 AFL-NFL MERGER)

1991

DIVISION CHAMPIONSHIPS (SINCE 1970 AFL-NFL MERGER)

1983, 1991, 1993

KEY COACHES

Buddy Parker (1951–56): 47–23–2,
   3–1 (playoffs)
George Wilson (1957–64):
   53–45–6, 2–0 (playoffs)

KEY PLAYERS *(position, seasons with team)*

Lem Barney (DB, 1967–77)
Jack Christiansen (DB, 1951–58)
Dutch Clark (QB/K, 1931–38)
Lou Creekmur (OL, 1950–59)
Calvin Johnson (WR, 2007–15)
Alex Karras (DT, 1958–70)
Dick Lane (DB, 1960–65)
Yale Lary (DB/P, 1952–53, 1956–64)
Bobby Layne (QB, 1950–58)
Dick LeBeau (DB, 1959–72)
Barry Sanders (RB, 1989–98)
Charlie Sanders (TE, 1968–77)
Joe Schmidt (LB, 1953–65)
Billy Sims (RB, 1980–84)
Matthew Stafford (QB, 2009–)
Doak Walker (HB/K/P, 1950–55)
Alex Wojciechowicz (C/DE,
   1938–46)

HOME FIELDS

Ford Field (2002–)
Pontiac Silverdome (1975–2001)
Tiger Stadium (1938–39, 1941–74)
   Also known as Briggs Stadium
University of Detroit Stadium
   (1934–37, 1940)
Universal Stadium (1930–33)

* All statistics through 2018 season

QUOTES AND ANECDOTES

Byron "Whizzer" White, who would later become a justice on the US Supreme Court, played running back for Detroit in 1940 and 1941. In 1940 he became the first Lion to win the NFL rushing title with 514 yards. White was a football star at the University of Colorado. He was drafted fourth overall by the NFL's Pittsburgh Pirates in 1938. White led the league in rushing as a rookie that year with 567 yards. After he deferred a Rhodes Scholarship for a year after college, he enrolled at Hertford College in England in 1939. He returned to the NFL with Detroit in 1940. His last season with the Lions, and in the NFL, was in 1941. He entered the US Navy during World War II. After the war, he enrolled in Yale Law School rather than return to football. White practiced law in Denver, Colorado, and in 1962, he was appointed to the Supreme Court by President John F. Kennedy. White served on the court until his retirement in 1993. He died in 2002 at the age of 84.

Detroit quarterback Bobby Layne wasn't happy that the team brought in Tobin Rote to provide competition at quarterback in 1957. Layne had led the Lions to NFL titles in 1952 and 1953 and had a lot of pride. He was not going to let Rote simply take the quarterback job from him. "One time we had a tough game in Chicago and were splitting time," Layne recalled. "I got knocked groggy and, laying there on the ground, I looked over at the bench and saw Tobin standing up and getting ready. I told myself, 'Let's go, Bobby. There's Rote waiting to take your bread and butter.' So I got up."

When the Lions got new uniforms in 2017 they made only minor tweaks to the logo and number font. The biggest change was adding the initials "WCF" on the left sleeve. They honor William Clay Ford Sr., the longtime team owner, who died in 2014. The Lions had worn a patch with Ford's initials since he died, but the tribute was made permanent with the new uniforms. Ford, grandson of automobile pioneer Henry Ford, purchased the

GLOSSARY

contract
An agreement to play for a certain team.

coordinator
An assistant coach who is in charge of the offense or defense.

draft
A system that allows teams to acquire new players coming into a league.

hall of fame
A place built to honor noteworthy achievements by athletes in their respective sports.

Heisman Trophy
The award given yearly to the best player in college football.

juke
A deceptive move to get around an opponent.

playoffs
A set of games played after the regular season that decides which team is the champion.

retire
To end one's career.

rookie
A professional athlete in his or her first year of competition.

wild card
A team that makes the playoffs even though it did not win its division.

MORE
INFORMATION

BOOKS

Hall, Brian. *Detroit Lions*. Minneapolis, MN: Abdo Publishing, 2017.

Karras, Steven M. *Detroit Lions*. New York: AV2 by Weigl, 2018.

Lajiness, Katie. *Detroit Lions*. Minneapolis, MN: Abdo Publishing, 2017.

ONLINE RESOURCES

Booklinks
NONFICTION NETWORK
FREE! ONLINE NONFICTION RESOURCES

To learn more about the Detroit Lions, visit **abdobooklinks.com** or scan this QR code. These links are routinely monitored and updated to provide the most current information available.

PLACES TO VISIT

Detroit Lions Headquarters and Training Facility
222 Republic Dr.
Allen Park, MI 48101
313–262–2000
This is the year-round team headquarters for the Lions. The public can watch the team at open practice sessions during training camp here.

Pro Football Hall of Fame
2121 George Halas Dr. NW
Canton, OH 44708
330–456–8207
profootballhof.com

This hall of fame and museum highlights the greatest players and moments in the history of the NFL. People affiliated with the Lions who are enshrined include Dutch Clark, Bobby Layne, and Barry Sanders.

INDEX

Barney, Lem, 23
Blades, Bennie, 28
Brown, Lomas, 28

Caldwell, Jim, 39, 41
Christiansen, Jack, 18
Clark, Earl "Dutch," 12
Clark, Potsy, 12

Doran, Jim, 17

Flanagan, Ed, 24
Fontes, Wayne, 31–32

Gatski, Frank, 18

Harder, Pat, 14–16
Harrington, Joey, 36

Johnson, Calvin, 38–40
Johnson, John Henry, 18

Karras, Alex, 20–23
Krieg, Dave, 30

Lane, Dick "Night Train," 20
Lary, Yale, 18, 20
Layne, Bobby, 6–8, 13, 15, 17–19, 20, 32, 36, 41
LeBeau, Dick, 18, 23

Marinelli, Rod, 37
McMillin, Alvin "Bo," 14
Millen, Matt, 34–37
Mitchell, Scott, 30–32
Moore, Herman, 28–29
Murray, Eddie, 25

Parker, Buddy, 4–6, 14, 18–19
Patricia, Matt, 41
Perriman, Brett, 28

Richards, George A., 9, 12
Rogers, Charles, 36
Ross, Bobby, 32
Rote, Tobin, 4–8, 18

Sanders, Barry, 26–33, 40
Sanders, Charlie, 23
Schmidt, Joe, 18, 20
Schwartz, Jim, 38–39
Scroggins, Tracy, 28
Sims, Billy, 25, 28
Spielman, Chris, 28
Stafford, Matthew, 38–41
Stanfel, Dick, 18
Suh, Ndamukong, 39

Utley, Mike, 30

Walker, Doak, 13, 16–17, 18, 41
Walker, Wayne, 23–24
Williams, Mike, 36
Williams, Roy, 36
Wilson, George, 6, 18

ABOUT THE AUTHOR

William Meier has worked as an author and editor in the publishing industry